A Note from
Mary Pope Osborne About the

MAGIC TREE HOUSE®
FACT TRACKERS

When I write Magic Tree House® adventures, I love including facts about the times and places Jack and Annie visit. But when readers finish these adventures, I want them to learn even more. So that's why my husband, Will, and my sister, Natalie Pope Boyce, and I write a series of nonfiction books that are companions to the fiction titles in the Magic Tree House® series. We call these books Fact Trackers because we love to track the facts! Whether we're researching dinosaurs, pyramids, Pilgrims, sea monsters, or cobras, we're always amazed at how wondrous and surprising the real world is. We want you to experience the same wonder we do—so get out your pencils and notebooks and hit the trail with us. You can be a Magic Tree House® Fact Tracker, too!

Mary Pope Osborne

Here's what kids, parents, and teachers have to say about the Magic Tree House® Fact Trackers:

"They are so good. I can't wait for the next one. All I can say for now is prepare to be amazed!" —Alexander N.

"I have read every Magic Tree House book there is. The [Fact Trackers] are a thrilling way to get more information about the special events in the story." —John R.

"These are fascinating nonfiction books that enhance the magical time-traveling adventures of Jack and Annie. I love these books, especially *American Revolution*. I was learning so much, and I didn't even know it!" —Tori Beth S.

"[They] are an excellent 'behind-the-scenes' look at what the [Magic Tree House fiction] has started in your imagination! You can't buy one without the other; they are such a complement to one another." —Erika N., mom

"Magic Tree House [Fact Trackers] took my children on a journey from Frog Creek, Pennsylvania, to so many significant historical events! The detailed manuals are a remarkable addition to the classic fiction Magic Tree House books we adore!" —Jenny S., mom

"[They] are very useful tools in my classroom, as they allow for students to be part of the planning process. Together, we find facts in the [Fact Trackers] to extend the learning introduced in the fictional companions. Researching and planning classroom activities, such as our class Olympics based on facts found in *Ancient Greece and the Olympics*, help create a genuine love for learning!" —Paula H., teacher

Magic Tree House®
Fact Tracker

GHOSTS

A nonfiction companion to
Magic Tree House® #42:
A Good Night for Ghosts

by Mary Pope Osborne
and Natalie Pope Boyce

illustrated by Sal Murdocca

A STEPPING STONE BOOK™
Random House 🏠 New York

The Magic Tree House Fact Tracker series was formerly known as the
Magic Tree House Research Guide series.

Visit us on the Web!
MagicTreeHouse.com
www.randomhouse.com/kids

Educators and librarians, for a variety of teaching tools, visit us at
www.randomhouse.com/teachers

Library of Congress Cataloging-in-Publication Data
Osborne, Mary Pope.
Ghosts : a nonfiction companion to a good night for ghosts / by Mary Pope
Osborne and Natalie Pope Boyce ; illustrated by Sal Murdocca.
 p. cm. — (Magic tree house fact tracker)
"A Stepping Stone book."
Includes index.
"A nonfiction companion to Magic Tree House #42: A Good Night for Ghosts."
ISBN 978-0-375-84666-3 (trade) — ISBN 978-0-375-94666-0 (lib. bdg.)
1. Ghosts—Juvenile literature. I. Boyce, Natalie Pope. II. Murdocca, Sal, ill.
III. Title.
BF1461.O87 2011 133.1—dc22 2011006314

Printed in the United States of America
12 11 10 9

To Cyndi Pratt and Sheila Del Soldato
with love

Historical Consultant:

DAVID DELGADO SHORTER, Associate Professor of World Arts and Cultures, UCLA

Education Consultant:

HEIDI JOHNSON, Earth Science and Paleontology, Lowell Junior High School, Bisbee, Arizona

As always, very special thanks to the excellent folks at Random House: Gloria Cheng, Liam Hart, Mallory Loehr, Lisa Findlay, and especially to our wonderful editor, Diane Landolf.

GHOSTS

Contents

1. Ghosts   13

2. America's Most Haunted   29

3. Haunted Washington, D.C.   57

4. Spooky Great Britain   75

5. What Are Ghosts All About?   99

Doing More Research   104

Index   113

Dear Readers,

When we came back from our adventure in <u>A Good Night for Ghosts</u>, we had lots of questions. Do ghosts really exist? What are some of the most famous ghost stories?

To find out the answers, we had to be fact trackers!

First, we got some great books from the library. Later, when we started looking up ghosts on the computer, we found some websites that were not helpful. You might need to ask your parents or a teacher or librarian to help you find useful information on the computer. When we did find good

websites, we began by tracking the facts about ghosts in the United States. Our search then led us to Great Britain.

We learned so much. Being a fact tracker is fun. So get out your notebooks and your ghost hunters' gear, and let's get going!

Jack
Annie

1

Ghosts

It was a hot summer night near Wilmington, North Carolina, many years ago. Two girls were hiding in the bushes by the railroad tracks at the old Maco train station.

Almost everyone in North Carolina knew about the Maco Light. Stories about it began in the mid-1800s when a terrible accident took the life of a railroad conductor on the Maco train tracks. The man's name was Joe Baldwin. Part of his job was to walk the tracks at night with a lantern to make sure the train had stopped at the right place. Joe's head was cut off in the accident. Some said he was gripping the lantern in his hand when he died.

After Joe's death, people started to say they sometimes saw a ghostly light floating above the tracks. As the light moved forward, it seemed to sway back and forth. It was as if there were someone with a lantern looking for something. People believed that it was Joe Baldwin searching for his missing head.

When the girls heard this story, they wanted to see the Maco Light for themselves. Time passed slowly as they waited. The night was dark and still. Swarms of mosquitoes buzzed around their heads. They were almost ready to give up when suddenly they saw a dim light coming down the tracks toward them. It swung from side to side and got brighter as it drew closer. The girls leapt up in horror and ran for their lives! Years later, the tracks were torn up. No one has seen the Maco Light since.

Now the girls are grown women. Neither of them believes in ghosts. But after all these years, they still cannot explain what they saw. They say it was such a strange sight that it still sends chills down their backs. They have told the story of their encounter with the Maco Light many times.

Ghost Stories

Ghost stories have been around for thousands of years. Before books, television, and computers, nights could seem long. To entertain themselves, people sat around the fire and told stories. Scary stories were just part of the fun.

Today we can still read ghost stories written by the ancient Greeks and Romans thousands of years ago. They believed that

ghosts were spirits of people who had not had a proper burial after they had died. There is one famous Greek ghost story about dead warriors who still haunt a battlefield thousands of years after the battle.

The Greeks defeated the powerful Persian army at the <u>Battle of Marathon</u>. They lost fewer than 200 men; the Persians lost more than 6,000.

Another story is from the Roman writer Pliny the Younger, who lived about two thousand years ago. Pliny's tale sounds a lot like ghost stories today. It's about a strange house haunted at night by the sound of rattling chains and the ghost of an old man. The ghost cannot rest until it is given a proper burial.

Like the Greeks and Romans, the Japanese and Chinese have a history of ghost stories going back thousands of years. Today children in Japan listen to the same stories their grandparents did about ghosts called *yurei* (YOO-ray).

Many *yurei* are young women who have long black hair and look pale and ghostly. They appear dressed in white and rarely speak.

The ghosts don't have feet or legs and

appear to float rather than walk. Their hands hang limply at their sides. At times wisps of bright red and green fire hover near them.

The name <u>yurei</u> comes from two words: <u>yu</u>, which means "dim," and <u>rei</u>, which means "soul."

Llorona means "weeping woman" in Spanish.

Just about every country has its own favorite ghost stories. If you travel to Mexico, you might hear tales of *La Llorona*, the famous crying ghost. She is supposed to wander the countryside dressed in white, weeping for her drowned children.

In Africa and in many other parts of the world, children often hear stories about friendly ghosts who are the spirits of their ancestors.

What Exactly Are Ghosts?

Many people who believe in ghosts think they are the spirits of those who have died but who are not ready to leave this world for the next. Ghosts often appear at night. Sometimes they drift in clouds of cold white mist, like the *yurei*. And like the *yurei*, their faces are pale and they almost never speak. If they are not seen, they make their presence known by moving things about, making noises, and opening and closing doors.

Ghosts even walk through walls.

The place where a ghost appears is said to be *haunted*. In most stories, the spirits of the dead haunt areas where they have lived or died.

In many tales, ghosts are kind and helpful. Sometimes the ghosts need help before they can rest in peace. But other ghosts are just plain scary and seem to stick around for the fun of it.

One family in Charleston, South Carolina, claims that a woman's ghost has haunted their house for over a hundred years. They all report a trail of icy air as the gentle spirit glides from room to room.

Belief in Ghosts

In some cultures, ghosts play active roles in everyday life. Each year, the village of Malajpur in India holds a famous ghost busters' fair. Many travel to the fair because they believe that their bodies are haunted by ghosts. There are people at the fair who claim to be able to cure them of their problems.

The fair lasts a month. Over ten thousand people visit every year.

An Indian healer works to cure this woman of her ghosts.

A few years ago, some schools in India closed for a while. The children claimed there were too many ghosts in their classrooms! They needed a vacation from them.

23

Spain, Brazil, and other countries also celebrate the dead with festivals.

For hundreds of years, the Japanese and the Chinese have held ghost festivals. The festivals celebrate the spirits of their dead relatives. Families gather to tidy up their graves and then honor their loved ones with feasts. In some homes, places are set at the table for the dead and candles burn on family altars honoring the spirits of their loved ones.

In Mexico, there is a special day called "the Day of the Dead." Mexicans visit their relatives' graves and have feasts in their honor. They feel that the spirits of the dead are with them on this day. This custom goes back thousands of years.

Our Halloween is similar. Every October 31, children dress up like ghosts and scary creatures. This comes from an old custom in Ireland, where people thought spirits roamed the countryside that night.

24

Mexicans shop for skulls made out of sugar to celebrate the Day of the Dead.

We may not all agree on ghosts, but one thing is sure: ghosts are a mystery. Stories about them can be exciting, inspiring, and chilling. And who knows? Maybe your town or city has its own favorite ghost stories. In fact, there might be a haunted house right down the street!

Will-o'-the-Wisps

For hundreds of years, people have seen ghostly lights around swamps during the night. The lights seem to hover over the ground and drift from place to place. Years ago, people thought the lights were ghosts.

In ghost stories the lights were called *will-o'-the-wisps*. This strange name came about because people used bundles of straw called *wisps* to start their fires. The swamp lights looked like burning wisps of straw. People began to tell tales about a forest spirit named Will. They said that Will used magic lights to trick travelers into going in the wrong direction. He became known as Will of the wisp.

Another name for Will of the wisp is Jack O'Lantern.

Today scientists know that when gas from rotting plants in a swamp mixes with certain gases in the air, they burn and create a ghostly glow. The scientists believe that this explains will-o'-the-wisps.

Could there have been a swamp near the Maco train station? That would explain a lot!

2

America's Most Haunted

There has never been another city quite like New Orleans. Parts of the city have buildings that look like those in France and Spain. That's because before New Orleans became part of the United States in 1812, it was first owned by France and later by Spain. Over the years, people from Haiti (HAY-tee) and Africa also settled in the city. They brought a rich treasure of

Folklore is the stories and customs people pass down through the years by word of mouth.

African *folklore* with them. Another gift they gave New Orleans was a type of music called *jazz*, which has its roots in African music.

The air in New Orleans is hot and damp. The city sits between the Mississippi River and Lake Pontchartrain. Because of this, there is a huge danger of floods. Houses are sometimes built high off the ground for protection. Earthen banks called *levees* act as walls to keep the city from flooding.

All over New Orleans, creepy-looking hanging moss droops from the trees. Crumbling old mansions line many of the streets. New Orleans is the perfect setting for some great ghost stories. In fact, some people call it the most haunted city in America.

This typical old New Orleans house was once home to Anne Rice, who is a famous writer.

Cities of the Dead

Folks in New Orleans call their graveyards "cities of the dead." That's because they have to bury the dead aboveground. The earth is so soggy that in rainy weather, coffins buried underground used to float to the surface. To solve this problem, many people are buried in tombs or in structures called *vaults*.

 This man leads one of many ghost tours of New Orleans.

Visitors walk down winding paths overgrown with moss and weeds. Silent tombs sit on either side of the walkways. During the holidays, candles cast ghostly shadows on the graves.

New Orleans has over forty-two cemeteries, but St. Louis Cemetery No. 1 is one of the most famous. It is said to be haunted by the ghost of an African American woman named Marie Laveau. When Marie died in the 1800s, many believed she had magical powers. People said she could summon up spirits and even make magic potions.

Marie Laveau

The type of magic Marie practiced is called voodoo. It comes from Haiti and Africa.

Legend has it that Marie's ghost appears as either a crow or a big black dog that runs through the cemetery. Sometimes visitors mark the tomb where Marie is supposed to be buried with three

large X's in hopes of having good luck. And for extra good luck, they turn around three times as well. (Just remember: it's against the law to mark up the tombs.)

Ghosts of the French Quarter

The oldest and most famous part of New Orleans is called the *French Quarter*. The French built many buildings there before Louisiana became part of the United States. New Orleans has a law that no one can tear down any of these wonderful, but sometimes spooky, old buildings. When you wander through the French Quarter, it's not hard to see why many famous ghost stories take place there.

Bourbon Street is the most famous street in the French Quarter.

Marie's daughter lived in this house,
which is now a voodoo shop.

Marie Laveau lived in the French
Quarter. People say that her ghost drifts
down St. Ann Street dressed in a white
gown with a handkerchief tied in seven
knots around her neck. A man once claimed

Marie's ghost hit him in the nose when he was in a drugstore. The victim said that her ghost asked him who she was. When he said he did not know, she gave him a good, hard punch!

There are other ghostly sightings in the French Quarter as well. People claim that the ghost of a woman sometimes sits on the roof of a house on Royal Street. They've named her "Julie, the Creole lady." The story goes that Julie died from grief because a young Frenchman would not marry her. Julie climbed up to the roof of her house and died overnight from the cold.

The Death Tree

Other famous French Quarter ghosts include those of a Turkish sultan and his family. In the 1800s, the sultan rented a huge house called the Gardette-LaPretre House for his big family and their servants. One dark and stormy night, intruders slipped in and murdered everyone.

The murderers buried the sultan in a

shallow grave underneath a tree in the courtyard. They were never caught, and no one ever knew why they murdered the family.

Gardette-LaPretre House

For years, people reported hearing Turkish music coming from the house. They also reported screams and ghostly figures around the tree.

Ghosts of the Civil War

Another haunted house in the French Quarter belonged to General Beauregard (BO-ruh-gard), who fought in the Civil War in the mid-1800s. Folks say that around two

General Beauregard

There are supposed to be ghost dogs and ghost cats haunting the house as well.

o'clock in the morning, the ghosts of the general and his soldiers haunt the ballroom.

At first, the men appear in fine uniforms. Then suddenly their clothes turn into bloody rags. Terrible wounds cover their bodies, and the sounds of battle begin to rumble through the house. Today General Beauregard's house is a museum that is not open at night!

Beauregard-Keyes House

Jean Lafitte's Blacksmith Shop

Jean Lafitte, a pirate, really looked the part. He was tall, dark, and handsome and was popular with the ladies. But most of all, Jean was daring. In the early 1800s, he and his band of pirates attacked and robbed ships up and down the coast from Texas to Louisiana. Yet Jean had a good side, too. He and his brother helped the United States in naval battles against the British in the War of 1812 and in the Battle of New Orleans in 1815.

Jean Lafitte

In 1823, Jean Lafitte attacked a Spanish ship. In the return fire, Jean was wounded and died. He was buried at sea.

Jean and his brother owned a blacksmith shop in the French Quarter. There is a rumor that he buried his treasure there under the fireplace. Today Lafitte's Blacksmith Shop is a popular bar. It's one of the oldest buildings in the French Quarter. Inside the dark and crumbling rooms, candles flicker. On cool days, a fire in the fireplace gives off a dim glow. People have noticed a lot of strange happenings at Lafitte's.

Jean himself sometimes appears. Some say he leans against the wall looking very cross and twirling his black mustache. Others report that he is clean-shaven and vanishes the minute anyone spots him.

Jean Lafitte's blacksmith shop was built before 1772.

45

There are other weird things at Lafitte's. People claim that glowing red eyes from the fireplace seem to be glaring at them. It's guessed that the eyes belong to the angry spirit of someone Jean left behind to guard his treasure.

What, Marie again?

Yes! There are reports that people have seen Marie Laveau's face in a mirror at Lafitte's. She's everywhere!

In other rooms, lights seem to turn themselves off and on. And people say that at times unseen hands have tapped them on the shoulder!

New Orleans is not the only place where Jean's ghost hangs out. Some claim to have seen it at a plantation house outside of town. And his ghost has also been spotted in places along the Texas coast. Everyone agrees that Jean really gets around!

Arnaud's Ghost

Restaurants in New Orleans have their share of strong-willed ghosts. Arnaud Cazenave was a Frenchman who owned a popular restaurant called *Arnaud's*. Arnaud was always very strict with his staff. He demanded the best, and it paid off. Years after his death, Arnaud's remains one of the most popular restaurants in town.

Arnaud Cazenave opened his restaurant in 1918.

Arnaud's daughter took over after his death. Her ghost seems to be haunting the place as well!

When Arnaud died, some really strange things began to happen. If waiters put forks, knives, or napkins in the wrong place, they would later find the utensils back in their proper order. Bartenders claimed that during the

48

night, someone seemed to tidy up the bar. And once when a bookkeeper was working alone around midnight, an icy blast of air blew through the bar. The man, who was usually very calm, ran out the door as fast as he could!

Some cooks say they still feel Arnaud's presence hovering around as they cook. At times, he appears to be smiling. But that doesn't fool them. Arnaud will let them know when they've made a mistake!

Le Petit Théâtre du Vieux Carré

Le Petit Théâtre du Vieux Carré is in an old building that has been standing since the late 1700s. According to legend, it is packed full of ghosts. Sometimes the ghosts of dead actors turn up. People claim they sometimes hear piano music in the theater, but no one can trace the sound. And sometimes icy gusts of wind blow the curtains back and forth for no reason at all.

The staff claims that the ghost of a well-dressed gentleman sometimes sits in the audience. They say he smells like fine pipe tobacco and expensive cologne. If the gentleman claps, the play will be a success. Actors always hope that someone will spot the gentleman ghost clapping away when the curtains go down.

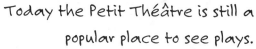

Today the Petit Théâtre is still a popular place to see plays.

Other ghosts may be haunting the theater as well. There have been sightings of soldiers in Civil War uniforms wandering about the lobby. One handsome young officer likes to look at himself in the mirror.

51

Not only does New Orleans have the most haunted bar, it also has the most haunted restaurants and the most haunted houses and theaters. No wonder people call it the most haunted city in America!

Jack and Annie's Guide to Ghost Hunting

Did you know there are people who make their living hunting ghosts? Sometimes strange things happen in a house. Objects appear to move around by themselves and noises and strange sights keep the owners awake at night. If people get really worried, they can call in professional ghost hunters to try to solve their problems.

The investigators bring their tools with them. There are thermometers to see if the air gets cold in different parts of the rooms. They also bring all kinds of cameras to catch any ghostly images that might appear and tape recorders to capture ghostly sounds.

The ghost hunters usually measure the distance between objects in a room to see if they change position. Then they take out their notebooks and record their research. Before they leave, they offer suggestions to the owners or maybe just assure them that there is nothing to worry about at all.

Does this sound like someone else we know?

3

Haunted Washington, D.C.

Did you know that the White House is said to be haunted? There are many reports of ghostly happenings there. Some folks say they've heard President Thomas Jefferson playing the violin. Jefferson was our third president. He died almost two hundred years ago! Others claim that the ghost of Abigail Adams, the wife of President John Adams, washes her clothes in the East

Room. Abigail died even before Jefferson did.

Gardeners in the Rose Garden have the feeling that Dolley Madison watches as they work. Dolley's husband, James Madison, was the fourth president of the United States. Dolley planted the first Rose Garden at the White House. Gardeners say that her ghost gets *very* cranky if they take out even one rosebush.

There are other mysterious goings-on too. White House staffers say that doors open and close when no one is there, lights turn themselves on and off, and icy currents of air float through the rooms.

Abraham Lincoln: The Polite Ghost

On the night of April 14, 1865, Abraham Lincoln and his wife went to Ford's Theatre to watch a play. A man crept up behind him and fired a bullet into his head. Lincoln died the following day.

The man who shot President Lincoln was an actor named John Wilkes Booth.

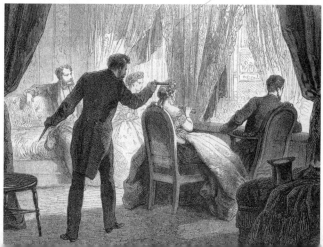

Presidents Theodore Roosevelt, Herbert Hoover, and Harry Truman all heard a strange knocking at their doors.

Many people think that Abraham Lincoln's ghost still haunts the White House. It is supposed to be a very polite ghost who always knocks before entering a room.

President Coolidge's wife thought she saw Lincoln's ghost staring out a window in the Oval Office. His hands were clasped behind his back as he gazed sadly toward the Potomac River.

One night a White House worker was checking an upstairs bedroom when he thought he saw Lincoln sitting on his bed, taking off his shoes. And early one morning, a White House usher saw Lincoln sitting in front of his old office. When the worker blinked, the ghost disappeared.

President Reagan's daughter Maureen

said that her dog refused to go into the Lincoln Bedroom. It just stood at the door and barked.

The most famous sighting of Lincoln was by Queen Wilhelmina of the Netherlands when she was visiting President Roosevelt in 1945. The queen heard a quiet knock on her bedroom door. She opened it, and there stood Abraham Lincoln in his top hat and dark suit. Some reports say the poor queen fainted dead away!

Amy Carter was nine when her father came to the White House.

Amy Carter's Prank

Amy Carter, President Carter's daughter, knew all about the White House ghosts.

One night she and a friend slept in the Lincoln Bedroom. They waited patiently for Lincoln's ghost to appear. Sadly, despite all the stories they'd heard, he never showed up.

Then Amy decided to scare some of the staff. She and another girl climbed into a laundry cart filled with linen that someone had left in an elevator. They carefully covered themselves up. The girls pushed the elevator button up to the second floor. When the elevator got there, a White House worker opened the door. The girls leapt out of the laundry basket and yelled, "Boo!" Reports say that the poor White House worker almost fainted . . . just like Queen Wilhelmina!

The White House is not the only haunted place in Washington. People claim that a lot of other buildings have some strange things going on in them as well.

To Do at the White House

Tell President Jefferson he plays
    really well.

Don't dig up rosebushes!

Watch out! Dolley's dancing!

Open if Abraham Lincoln knocks.

Don't faint . . . just chat with him.

If you dare, turn the page
to take a ghost tour of
Washington, D.C., with us!

The Ghost Cat of the Capitol Building

The Capitol Building is at the top of Capitol Hill near the White House. It is where the nation's lawmakers do much of their work. During the day, it's as busy as a beehive.

Workers say that at night, when all is quiet, things can get exciting down in the basement. At one time, they kept cats there to get rid of rats. Today there are no cats except for one . . . the famous ghost cat of the Capitol Building.

Some say a terrible cat haunts the basement's halls and tunnels. They say that at first the cat is the size of a kitten. But as it creeps closer, it grows *really* big . . . as big as a tiger! Its eyes burn like coals; its purr becomes a fierce growl. Legend has it that seeing the cat means that something bad is about to happen. (Yeah, like maybe a heart attack!)

The National Theatre's Friendly Ghost

For more than one hundred years, a friendly ghost is said to have haunted the National Theatre. It is supposed to be the ghost of a popular actor named John McCullough, who died in the 1800s. John was killed in a fight with another actor. His body was buried beneath the dirt floor in the cellar. Workers recently found a rusty pistol under the basement floor, but so far, no one has found any remains.

Some say that John's ghost checks the scenery and the props to make sure everything is all right. One actor even swore he saw John sitting in the audience.

The most dramatic sighting was by John's fellow actor in the late 1800s. He claimed that John's ghost appeared on-stage. When the actor called out his name, the ghost quietly left.

No one is sure where John McCullough is really buried. But if you work at the National Theatre, it's nice to think John is helping you out. And you don't even have to pay him!

The Omni Shoreham Hotel

The Omni Shoreham is an elegant hotel in Washington, D.C. In the 1930s, Henry Doherty and his wife moved into several rooms there. Along with them were their daughter, Helen, and their housekeeper, Juliette Brown. One day a hotel worker discovered Juliette's dead body lying in her bed. Not long after, Helen Doherty also died in her bedroom.

After the Dohertys moved out in 1973, very strange things began to happen in their old rooms. Guests reported that someone had moved the TV and the lamps. They also complained about strange noises and icy gusts of wind. The staff wondered if the ghosts of Helen and Juliette were still hanging around.

The hotel decided to call the Dohertys'

rooms "The Ghost Suite." They are now among the most popular rooms in the hotel. But are *you* ready to spend the night there?

The Octagon House

The Octagon House may be Washington's most haunted house. A rich man named John Tayloe owned it in the early 1800s. Two of his daughters died in separate falls down the long staircase.

Today their unhappy ghosts are supposed to haunt their old home. People report seeing the shadow from a burning candle moving up the stairs. Then the sound of a scream rings out, as if someone were falling.

James and Dolley Madison lived in the Octagon House for several years. Dolley's ghost is said to leave behind a trail of lilac perfume. People sometimes think they see her dancing in the ballroom.

At times, workers report the sounds of carriages rolling up to the door and strange footprints tracking across the floors. Some even say they smell food coming from the kitchen.

Today the Octagon House is in the process of being restored so it can be opened to the public. Someday, visitors might be able to spot Dolley Madison dancing her heart out.

4

Spooky Great Britain

Across the ocean, the Queen of England has the same problem that presidents of the United States have—only her problem is with ghosts in her palace! What else would you expect in a country with graveyards, old churches, ancient castles, and creaking mansions all over the place? Great Britain's history is rich and exciting. Over the years, there have been fierce battles, Viking invasions, and colorful kings and queens. All of

The village of Pluckley claims to have twelve very active ghosts!

these things make for wonderful ghost stories.

Many of the first settlers in America came from this part of the world. Today their folklore is still an important part of the culture of the United States.

Some of the earliest English ghost stories go back two thousand years, to a time when Roman armies ruled the land. They built forts where the towns of York and Chester sit today. The ghosts of Roman soldiers are said to haunt both cities.

Well, actually, he said he never saw their feet, just their upper bodies. But they looked like they were marching!

Some say that Roman soldiers haunt the basement of the Treasury House in York. A plumber working there claimed that a group of Roman soldiers, armed with swords, shields, and spears, marched out of one wall to the sound of a

76

trumpet. Then the men marched quickly across the room and through the opposite wall.

Windsor Castle

Windsor Castle, a private home of Queen Elizabeth II, has more than its share of ghostly tales. The queen sometimes leaves Buckingham Palace in London to spend

time there. Windsor Castle is over nine hundred years old. Today it's the largest castle in the world that has people living in it. It also might be the most haunted castle there is.

Windsor Castle

Some of the kings and queens who lived there sometimes turn up as ghosts. People declare they hear King Henry VIII groaning and moaning as he drags himself up and down the stairs. (During his lifetime, Henry had terrible sores on his legs.) His daughter Elizabeth I seems to be haunting the castle

Witnesses claim that Elizabeth wears a black dress and is very, very grand.

as well. According to some in the royal family, they hear Elizabeth's high heels clicking across the wooden floors. Soon her ghost appears and walks proudly through the library. King George III's ghost has been spotted gazing sadly out a window. And poor King Charles I, whose head was cut off, shows up in the library and in one of the other houses on the grounds.

But that's not all. Some say bells in the Curfew Tower ring by themselves. People claim that when they do, the air in the tower gets very chilly. And then there is the ghost of Herne the Hunter, which wanders in the Windsor woods. Herne's been there a long time. Henry VIII claimed to have seen him and that was over four hundred years ago!

Oh, and let's not forget the castle's

kitchen: the ghost of a man leading a horse walks right through the wall there. And there's the ghost of a little girl who stands by a Christmas tree. And then there are reports that sometimes the voice of a boy shouts, "I don't want to go riding today!" You get the idea: Windsor Castle may be extra-super-haunted!

A terrible fire burned much of the castle in 1992. It took five years to repair.

Tower of London

Anne Boleyn and the Terrible Tower

Each day, visitors tour the famous Tower of London. The tower has been around for over nine hundred years. It has been a fort, a palace, and a prison. Over the years, the tower has held many well-known prisoners. Whenever kings or queens suspected people of plotting against them, they put them in the tower. Some unlucky prisoners were hanged or had their heads chopped off.

Ghosts are supposed to be just about everywhere, walking around the tower grounds and halls or just staring hopelessly out windows.

Anne and Henry's daughter, Elizabeth I, became one of the most powerful rulers Britain has ever had.

The most well-known ghost is that of Anne Boleyn. Anne was the second wife of King Henry VIII. He married her in 1533. Altogether King Henry had six wives. One died after an illness, two (including Anne) had their heads cut off, and the king divorced two others. Henry's last wife had the good luck to live longer than he did.

Anne Boleyn

Henry VIII

When the king decided that Anne was not the wife he wanted, he put her in the tower. Then he ordered that her head be chopped off. Some people declare that Anne's headless ghost walks back and forth in front of the chapel right below the room where she once lived.

One strange story about her ghost comes from the 1800s. A tower guard passed the locked chapel at night. He noticed a light coming from there. Climbing up a ladder, the guard looked through the window and saw an amazing sight. A parade of knights and ladies led by Anne marched slowly down the aisle.

There is another legend about Anne Boleyn. Her house used to be on the grounds where Blickling Hall is today. Blickling Hall is one of England's great houses. It's said that every year, on the date of her death, Anne's ghost arrives in a coach driven by a headless driver and pulled by headless horses.

The Grey Lady of Glamis Castle

Glamis (GLAHMZ) Castle is in Scotland. It was built in the 1400s by a powerful Scottish family. In the 1500s, the King of Scotland turned against the Lord of Glamis and his wife, Lady Janet Douglas. Neither she nor her husband was guilty of any wrongdoing. The king threw Lord Glamis in prison. After Lord Glamis died, the king ordered the death of Lady Janet.

Parts of Glamis Castle are open to visitors.

People believe that Lady Janet still haunts Glamis Castle. They call her ghost the Grey Lady of Glamis. According to legend, people see the Grey Lady floating over the clock tower in a red glowing light. Her ghost also appears in the chapel.

To this day, no one is ever allowed to sit in Lady Janet's old chapel seat.

Glamis Castle has other ghosts as well. A sad girl was once spotted looking out a window. When someone tried to speak to her, she disappeared as if someone pulled her back from the window.

Noises like thumps and knocking have also been reported. People have also seen the ghost of a little servant boy near an upstairs bedroom. If you ever get to Scotland, you just might want to visit Glamis Castle. When you get to the chapel, don't take the Grey Lady's seat!

Stonehenge

Stonehenge

Stonehenge is about eighty miles from London. It is one of the most famous sights in the world.

Almost everyone who visits agrees that this ancient place has an amazing sense of mystery.

It looks as if a giant built Stonehenge. Stones weighing as much as fifty tons stand upright in large circles. Almost five thousand years ago, an ancient people dragged these stones from great distances. How did people who had very few tools get them there? Nobody knows exactly how or why they did it.

Experts say that ancient people at Stonehenge used tools made out of deer antlers and cattle bones.

Scientists at Stonehenge have uncovered the bones of many people who were sick or injured. They now believe that Stonehenge might have been a place where people came to get well. In the middle of Stonehenge, there used to be a circle of special rocks called bluestone. People believed that bluestone had healing powers and traveled long distances to find relief from their problems. Over the years, people have chipped away at the stones. They thought that if they had a piece of bluestone with them, they would get well. There used to be eighty bluestones at Stonehenge. Today only about a third remain.

Experts say that the bluestones came from 250 miles away in Wales. There are old stories that Merlin's magic brought the stones from so far away. But how people actually got them to Stonehenge is still a mystery.

Some scientists think the stones were first dragged on sleds with rollers. Then they were loaded onto rafts and floated on water down to the site.

Ghosts of the ancient people who built Stonehenge are said to haunt the grounds.

Legend has it that people have spotted them standing next to two large stones called the Heelstone and the Altar Stone.

Turn the page to find out what we'd be like as ghosts!

If We Were Ghosts . . .

If we were ghosts, we could:

walk through walls

scare people

float above houses

make scary noises

glow like candles

float like snow

never take a bath

stay up all night

5

What Are Ghosts All About?

After thousands of years, many people still believe in ghosts. People write books and make movies about them. There are reports of ghosts in the pyramids, ghosts in churches, ghosts in forests and in lakes and mountains. There are stories of ghost dogs, ghost cats, ghost ships, and even ghost hats and airplanes!

Besides being great fun to tell, ghost

stories often try to explain things we don't understand.

What *was* that noise in the other room? Is there something under my bed or in my closet? Do ghosts really exist?

We ask ourselves these questions and sometimes there are no answers. Or are there? People who have researched ghosts say there might be good reasons we hear and see strange things. Many times they find that natural events cause our ghostly fears. Here is what they say:

1. Rats, mice, squirrels, and other animals can make a lot of thumping and bumping sounds in a house.

2. Sometimes wooden floors creak and furnaces make noises when they turn on and off.

3. Houses sometimes settle a little lower

into the ground. This can cause strange thumps and creaks.

4. Small earthquakes or underground pipes or water can cause the earth to move and doors to open and close.

5. Swamp gas, changes in temperature, and car headlights moving in and out of sight at night can cause light to look ghostly and mysterious.

6. Air currents that are part of regular temperature changes can create cold breezes.

7. Problems with the electricity can cause the lights and the TV to turn on and off.

What do you think? Do you believe in ghosts? There are still many things we cannot explain. When we don't understand something, we often create stories about it. Ghosts remain a mystery. Maybe they always will. Remember, we've been telling stories about them for thousands of years.

The women who saw the Maco Light just can't get it out of their heads. It still bothers them and makes them wonder

what they actually saw. Whenever they talk about their experience, people listening get goose bumps. Everyone agrees that it's a really great story.

Doing More Research

There's a lot more you can learn about ghosts. The fun of research is seeing how many different sources you can explore.

Books

Most libraries and bookstores have lots of books about ghosts.

Here are some things to remember when you're using books for research:

1. You don't have to read the whole book. Check the table of contents and the index to find the topics you're interested in.

2. Write down the name of the book. When you take notes, make sure you write

down the name of the book in your note-book so you can find it again.

3. Never copy exactly from a book.
When you learn something new from a book, put it in your own words.

4. Make sure the book is <u>nonfiction</u>.
Some books tell make-believe stories about ghosts. Make-believe stories are called *fiction*. They're fun to read, but not good for research.

Research books have facts and tell true stories. They are called *nonfiction*. A traditional story that has been repeated often is *folklore*. A librarian or teacher can help you make sure the books you use for research are nonfiction or folklore.

Here are some good nonfiction books about ghosts in folklore:

- *Brave Bear and the Ghosts: A Sioux Legend* by Gloria Dominic

- *The Ghost Catcher* by Martha Hamilton and Mitch Weiss

- *Ghosts* by Jacqueline Laks Gorman

- *Ghosts! Ghostly Tales from Folklore* by Alvin Schwartz

- *Mexican Ghost Tales of the Southwest* by Alfred Avila and Kat Avila

- *Who's Haunting the White House? The President's Mansion and the Ghosts Who Live There* by Jeff Belanger

Museums and Landmarks

Many famous places are said to be haunted. Some towns even give ghost tours, so look around! These places can help you learn more about ghosts and ghost stories.

When you go to a museum or famous site:

1. Be sure to take your notebook!
Write down anything that catches your interest. Draw pictures, too!

2. Ask questions.
There are almost always people at museums who can help you find what you're looking for.

3. Check the calendar.
Many museums have special events and activities just for kids!

Here are a few ghostly places to visit:

- Alamo (San Antonio)

- Alcatraz Island (San Francisco)

- Beauregard-Keyes House and Garden Museum (New Orleans)

- Capitol Building (Washington, D.C.)

- Ford's Theatre (Washington, D.C.)

- Octagon House (Washington, D.C.)

- White House (Washington, D.C.)

DVDs

There are some great nonfiction DVDs about ghosts. As with books, make sure the DVDs you watch for research are nonfiction!

Check your library or video store for these and other nonfiction titles about ghosts:

- *Castle Ghosts of the British Isles*
  from Kultur Video

- *Stonehenge Decoded*
  from National Geographic

- *The Tower*
  from Koch Vision

- *Unexplained—Hauntings*
  from History Channel

The Internet

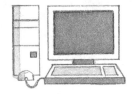

Many websites have facts about ghosts and ghost stories. Some also have games and activities that can help make learning about ghosts even more fun.

Ask your teacher or your parents to help you find more websites like these:

- castleofspirits.com/glamis2.html

- castles-of-britain.com/castle94.htm

- channel.nationalgeographic.com/episode /stonehenge-decoded-3372

- ehow.com/how_2132061_ghost-hunting -washington-dc.html

- legendsofamerica.com/gh-lallorona.html

- nationalgeographic.com/features/97/castles/enter.html

- nationaltheatre.org/location/ghost.htm

Good luck!

Index

Adams, Abigail,
57–58
Adams, John, 57
Africa, 20, 29–30, 33
Arnaud's, 47–49

Baldwin, Joe, 13–14
Beauregard,
General, 41–42
Beauregard-Keyes
House, 41–42
Blickling Hall, 88
bluestone, 93–94
Boleyn, Anne, 83–88
Booth, John Wilkes,
59
Bourbon Street, 36
Brazil, 24
Brown, Juliette, 70

Buckingham Palace,
78

Capitol Building, 67
Carter, Amy, 63–64
Carter, Jimmy, 63
cats, ghosts of, 42,
67, 99
Cazenave, Arnaud,
47–49
Charles I, 81
Charleston, South
Carolina, 22
China, 18, 24
Civil War, 41, 51
Coolidge, Calvin, 60

Day of the Dead, 24,
25

Death Tree, 40

dogs, ghosts of, 34,
42, 99

Doherty, Helen, 70

Doherty, Henry, 70

Douglas, Lady
Janet, 88–90

Elizabeth I, 80–81,
84

Elizabeth II, 75, 78

England, *see* Great
Britain

folklore, 30, 34, 76;
see also ghosts,
stories about

Ford's Theatre, 59

France, 29

French Quarter,
36–47

Gardette-LaPretre

House, 39–41

George III, 81

ghosts
belief in, 22–25, 99
fairs and festivals
about, 22–25
hunting for, 54–55
stories about,
13–20, 25, 30, 36,
76, 99–103

Glamis Castle,
88–90

Great Britain, 75–95

Greece, 16–17, 18

Grey Lady of
Glamis, 88–90

Haiti, 29, 33

Halloween, 24

Henry VIII, 80, 81,
84–85

Herne the Hunter,
81

Hoover, Herbert, 60

India, 22–23
Ireland, 24

Jack O'Lantern, 27
Japan, 18–19, 24
jazz, 30
Jefferson, Thomas,
    57, 58, 65
Julie, the Creole
    lady, 39

Lafitte, Jean, 43–47
Lafitte's Blacksmith
    Shop, 44–47
Laveau, Marie,
    33–35, 37–38, 46
levees, 30
Lincoln, Abraham,
    59–65
Llorona, La, 20
London, 78, 83–88, 92

Maco Light, 13–15,
    27, 102–103
Madison, Dolley, 58,
    65, 72–73
Madison, James, 58,
    72
Marathon, Battle of,
    17
McCullough, John,
    68–69
Merlin, 94
Mexico, 20, 24
Mississippi River, 30

National Theatre,
    68–69
New Orleans, 29–52
    Battle of, 43
    graveyards of,
    31–35

Octagon House,
    72–73

Omni Shoreham
    Hotel, 70–71
Oval Office, 60

Petit Théâtre du
    Vieux Carré, Le,
    50–51
Pliny the Younger,
    18
Pluckley, 76
Pontchartrain,
    Lake, 30
Potomac River, 60

Reagan, Maureen,
    60–61
Reagan, Ronald, 60
Rice, Anne, 31
Rome, 16, 18, 76–77
Roosevelt, Franklin,
    62
Roosevelt, Theodore,
    60

St. Louis Cemetery
    No. 1, 33–35
Scotland, 88–90
Spain, 24, 29, 44
Stonehenge, 92–95

Tayloe, John, 72
Texas, 43, 47
Tower of London,
    83–87
Treasury House,
    76–77
Truman, Harry, 60

voodoo, 33, 37

War of 1812, 43
Washington, D.C.,
    57–73
White House, 57–65,
    67
Wilhelmina, Queen,
    62, 64

will-o'-the-wisps,
26–27
Wilmington, North
Carolina, 13
Windsor Castle,
78–82

York, 76–77
yurei, 18–19, 21

Photographs courtesy of:

Have you read the adventure that
matches up with this book?

Don't miss Magic Tree House® #42

A Good Night for Ghosts

Jack and Annie are on their second mission to
find—and inspire—artists to bring happiness to
millions. After traveling to New Orleans, Jack
and Annie come head to head with some real
ghosts, as well as discover the world of jazz
when they meet a young Louis Armstrong!

If you like Magic Tree House® #46:
Dogs in the Dead of Night,
you'll love finding out the facts
behind the fiction in

Magic Tree House® Fact Tracker

DOG HEROES

A nonfiction companion to
Dogs in the Dead of Night

It's Jack and Annie's very own guide
to dog heroes!

Available now!

Magic Tree House® Books

#1: DINOSAURS BEFORE DARK
#2: THE KNIGHT AT DAWN
#3: MUMMIES IN THE MORNING
#4: PIRATES PAST NOON
#5: NIGHT OF THE NINJAS
#6: AFTERNOON ON THE AMAZON
#7: SUNSET OF THE SABERTOOTH
#8: MIDNIGHT ON THE MOON
#9: DOLPHINS AT DAYBREAK
#10: GHOST TOWN AT SUNDOWN
#11: LIONS AT LUNCHTIME
#12: POLAR BEARS PAST BEDTIME
#13: VACATION UNDER THE VOLCANO
#14: DAY OF THE DRAGON KING
#15: VIKING SHIPS AT SUNRISE
#16: HOUR OF THE OLYMPICS
#17: TONIGHT ON THE *TITANIC*
#18: BUFFALO BEFORE BREAKFAST
#19: TIGERS AT TWILIGHT
#20: DINGOES AT DINNERTIME
#21: CIVIL WAR ON SUNDAY
#22: REVOLUTIONARY WAR ON WEDNESDAY
#23: TWISTER ON TUESDAY
#24: EARTHQUAKE IN THE EARLY MORNING
#25: STAGE FRIGHT ON A SUMMER NIGHT
#26: GOOD MORNING, GORILLAS
#27: THANKSGIVING ON THURSDAY
#28: HIGH TIDE IN HAWAII

Merlin Missions
#29: CHRISTMAS IN CAMELOT
#30: HAUNTED CASTLE ON HALLOWS EVE
#31: SUMMER OF THE SEA SERPENT
#32: WINTER OF THE ICE WIZARD

#33: CARNIVAL AT CANDLELIGHT
#34: SEASON OF THE SANDSTORMS
#35: NIGHT OF THE NEW MAGICIANS
#36: BLIZZARD OF THE BLUE MOON
#37: DRAGON OF THE RED DAWN
#38: MONDAY WITH A MAD GENIUS
#39: DARK DAY IN THE DEEP SEA
#40: EVE OF THE EMPEROR PENGUIN
#41: MOONLIGHT ON THE MAGIC FLUTE
#42: A GOOD NIGHT FOR GHOSTS
#43: LEPRECHAUN IN LATE WINTER
#44: A GHOST TALE FOR CHRISTMAS TIME
#45: A CRAZY DAY WITH COBRAS
#46: DOGS IN THE DEAD OF NIGHT

Magic Tree House® Fact Trackers

DINOSAURS

KNIGHTS AND CASTLES

MUMMIES AND PYRAMIDS

PIRATES

RAIN FORESTS

SPACE

TITANIC

TWISTERS AND OTHER TERRIBLE STORMS

DOLPHINS AND SHARKS

ANCIENT GREECE AND THE OLYMPICS

AMERICAN REVOLUTION

SABERTOOTHS AND THE ICE AGE

PILGRIMS

ANCIENT ROME AND POMPEII

TSUNAMIS AND OTHER NATURAL DISASTERS

POLAR BEARS AND THE ARCTIC

SEA MONSTERS

PENGUINS AND ANTARCTICA

LEONARDO DA VINCI

GHOSTS

LEPRECHAUNS AND IRISH FOLKLORE

RAGS AND RICHES: KIDS IN THE TIME OF CHARLES DICKENS

SNAKES AND OTHER REPTILES

DOG HEROES

More Magic Tree House®

GAMES AND PUZZLES FROM THE TREE HOUSE